Tony's Birds

by MILLICENT E. SELSAM

Illustrated by Kurt Werth

A Science I CAN READ Book

HARPER & ROW, PUBLISHERS, NEW YORK, EVANSTON, AND LONDON

To Tony

Tony's Birds

"What a day!" said Tony.

He ran across the grass.

The sun was out.

The grass smelled good.

Tony went into his house.

"Let's go for a walk, Father," he said.

"All right. Let's go now,"

said his father.

Tony held his father's hand.

They walked down the road.

"What do you have in your other hand?"

asked Tony.

"Field glasses," said his father.

"If we see any birds on the way,

I can look at them with these."

"Oh," said Tony.

"I can look with my eyes!"

They walked along.

Then his father stopped.

He lifted the glasses to his eyes.

"There goes a blackbird," he said.

"Where?" asked Tony.

"It was on that pole," said his father.

"See, it just flew off."

Tony looked.

He saw the pole, but no bird.

They walked along.

His father lifted the glasses again.

"There goes a bluejay," said his father.

"Where?" asked Tony.

"Over there." His father pointed.

"It just flew into that tree."

Tony saw the tree, but no bird.

They walked along.

Then his father stood still.

"What now?" asked Tony.

"Do you see another bird?"

"No," said his father.

"I hear one. Listen."

11

Tony stood still.

He listened.

He heard a bird sing.

"That's a robin," said his father.

"How do you know?" asked Tony.

"A robin has his own song," said his father.

Tony was surprised.

"Is the robin's song different?
Does it sound different
from other bird songs?" asked Tony.

"Oh, yes," said his father.

"Does *every* kind of bird
have its own song?" asked Tony.

"Yes," said his father.

"Well," said Tony. "That's funny.
I thought all birds said 'Tweet.'"

Tony was quiet all the way home.

He was thinking.

"I did not see one bird.

I must have a good look at *one* bird."

The next morning Tony went to school.

At the corner, he waited for the bus.

He leaned against a tree.

Just then, a bird flew over his head
into the tree.

Tony looked up.

He didn't move at all.

He just stood there and looked.

The bird was gray.

It had a black cap.

It had a long tail.

"What kind of bird is that?" thought Tony.

"I wish my father were here."

All the way to school,

Tony said over and over,

"Gray, black cap, long tail."

16

When he got to school,

he put his books down.

Then he found a piece of paper.

He drew a gray bird with a long tail.

He colored the cap black.

That night, before dinner, Tony said,

"Father, I saw a bird.

It was gray all over.

It had a black cap.

And it had a long tail.

Here is a picture of it.

Do you know what it is?"

"I think I do," said Tony's father.

He went to the book shelf.

He picked out a book.

He turned the pages.

"Was it this one, Tony?" asked his father.

Tony looked.

There in the book was

a picture of his bird!

"This is a catbird," said his father.

Tony took the book in his hands.

"This is a better picture than mine.

Does this book have pictures

of all the birds?"

"Yes, Tony," said his father.

"It's called a *guide* book.

This book helps you to get to know birds."

"May I use it?" asked Tony.

"Of course," said his father.

The next day, Tony said, "Father,

I am going for a bird walk.

May I use your glasses?"

"All right," said his father.

His father put the strap

around Tony's neck.

The glasses came down to Tony's knees.

"I'll fix it," said his father.

He made the strap shorter.

23

Tony walked down the road.

He sat down on a big rock.

He put the glasses to his eyes.

He could not see a thing.

"I'll never see a bird

with these," he said.

He turned the little wheel
on the field glasses.
"Wow!" cried Tony.
The tree down the road
seemed to jump close.

The daisies across the road
seemed right in front of him.
Tony thought he could put his hand out
and touch them.

He took the glasses away from his eyes.

The tree was far away.

The daisies were back across the road.

26

Tony looked through the glasses again.

Just then, a catbird flew down

to the daisies.

"Oh!" he cried.

"This is why my father

could see all the birds."

The catbird looked very big.

Tony watched it.

The catbird cleaned its feathers

with its bill.

Tony put the glasses down.

How small the catbird looked!

"The next time I go for a bird walk
with my father," thought Tony,
"I'll be the one to see all the birds."

On Saturday Tony went for a bird walk

with his father.

Tony wore the glasses.

His father had the guide book

in his pocket.

They walked down the road.

Tony saw the first bird.

He put the glasses to his eyes.

"It's very big and blue," he said.

"And it has a black ring around its neck.
What is it?"

"Let's look it up," said his father.

They sat down on a rock.

They turned the pages of the bird book.

They passed over the pictures of ducks.

Tony's bird was not a duck.

It wasn't a goose or a swan.

Tony turned some more pages.
It was not a hawk.

It was not an eagle.

It was not an owl.

There were no blue woodpeckers.

It was not a bluebird.

Bluebirds did not have black rings

around their necks.

They turned some more pages.

"Stop!" cried Tony.

"There's my bird. It's a bluejay."

Then he turned to his father.

"This book is good. It works."

On Sunday, Tony went for a walk again.

This time he went alone.

He walked a long time.

Then he sat down on a rock

and looked around.

A bird flew into the tall weeds near him.

Tony sat very still.

What kind of bird was this?

It was brown on top.

It had a white breast.

There were brown stripes

on the white breast.

Tony watched.

The bird was eating seeds.

Tony stayed there till the bird flew away.

Then he went home.

He ran into the house.

He was saying, "Brown top, white breast,

brown stripes on the white."

He found the bird guide.

"This is funny," Tony said to himself.

"Here is a whole page of birds

that look like mine.

"They are all sparrows.

A whole page of sparrows."

Tony looked at each one.

One of these birds was his.

But which one?

Tony went to find his father.

"Father," he said, "can I take this book
with me tomorrow?"

"You may," said his father.

The next day Tony went to look
for his bird.

The bird guide was in his pocket.

The field glasses were around his neck.

Tony went to the same rock.

He sat down.

He waited.

Suddenly a bird flew down to the weeds.

Tony looked through the glasses.

But the sun was setting.

It was shining right into his eyes.

He could not see very much.

"I will have to get around to

the other side of that bird," he thought.

"Then I will be able to see."

Tony walked slowly—

a few steps at a time.

"If I walk fast, or run,

the bird will fly away,"

he said to himself.

Tony kept moving, very slowly.

At last he stopped.

He lifted his glasses slowly.

Now he could see.

The sun was behind him.

It was a sparrow.

But was it the same one he saw yesterday?

He looked again.

Crash! Bang!

A big dog jumped through the bushes.

The dog barked.

Tony looked at the dog.

"SSHHHHHH!" he said.

But it was too late.

His bird was gone.

Tony was mad.

The dog was Pal.

And right behind Pal

was Tony's friend, Ken.

"You dope!" Tony yelled.

"You scared my bird away!"

"What bird?" asked Ken.

"My bird!" yelled Tony.

"It took me so long to get

to where I could see it.

Now you've scared it away."

"I'm sorry, Tony. I didn't know
you were here. But I can show you
how to get that bird back."
Tony looked at Ken.
"Well, show me," he said.
First Ken sent his dog home.
Then he sat down next to Tony.

He put his hands to his mouth

and made funny noises.

"You look silly kissing your hand,"

said Tony.

But Ken just kept on.

"This is funny," thought Tony,

"but it won't bring my bird back."

But then a bird flew down

to the tall weeds.

Tony lifted his glasses.

Before he could get a good look,

another bird flew down to the weeds.

Ken was still making the funny noises.

Another bird came.

Then another.

"You are right, Ken," said Tony.

"The birds do like that noise."

He looked through the glasses.

The birds were sparrows.

They were brown on top.

They had white breasts.

There were brown stripes on the white.

They were his sparrows.

But what kind of sparrow were they?

Tony said to Ken, "Quick,

find the sparrow page."

Tony looked through the glasses

at the sparrows.

Then he looked at the pictures.

He looked at the birds again.

He looked at the pictures again.

"Oh," he said.

"These birds have a black spot

in the middle of their breasts."

"Let me look," said Ken.

He looked at the sparrows.

Then he picked up the book.

"It could be a song sparrow," Ken said.

Tony looked at the pictures.

"Here's another sparrow

with a black spot on its breast," he said.

"But that one has no stripes," said Ken.

"That's right," said Tony.

"These must be song sparrows."

"Say, Tony," said Ken. "This is some book. The pictures look just like the birds."

"That's what a bird guide is for," said Tony.

One day Tony's father said,

"Now I'll take you to a special place."

They walked into the woods.

They sat down near a brook.

They heard the water run over the stones.

They heard the wind in the trees.

"Listen," said Tony.

"Do you hear that?"

"I hear it," said Tony's father.

"It's the call of the ovenbird.

Do you hear it saying,

'Teacher, teacher, teacher'?"

"Yes!" said Tony. "I'd like to take

that teacher bird to school!"

After that, Tony went to the woods often.

He loved the call of the ovenbird.

One day he sat still for a very long time.

"I'm like a tree stump," he thought.

Just then, he saw the ovenbird.

It walked on little pink feet

   over the leaves

   over the logs

   to the brook.

It stood beside the brook.

It dipped its bill in the water.

Then it put its head back.

Tony watched.

When Tony got home, he said to his father,

"Do you know how a bird drinks?"

"No," said his father.

"Wait here," said Tony.

He ran to the kitchen.

He came back with a bowl of water.

"Watch," he said.

He filled his mouth with water.

Then he put his head back.

Goggle! Goggle! It didn't go down.

Tony coughed up the water.

"Well," he said,

"the ovenbird did it anyway."

"Did what?" said his father.

"The ovenbird put its bill in the water.

Then it put its head back.

It did that over and over."

"I've seen them do that," said his father.

"But I never thought about it."

"I guess birds can't swallow

the way we do," said Tony.

"I guess they have to put their heads back

to let the water run down their throats."

"You taught me something new today," said Tony's father.

"I'll teach you a lot more," cried Tony.

"I'm a teacher, teacher, teacher!
I'm going to know more about birds than anybody around."

"I hope you will," said Tony's father.